# AFTERMATH

# AFTERMATH

## JOHN RYAN

**To order additional copies of this book, contact:**
Xlibris Corporation
0-800-644-6988
www.xlibrispublishing.co.uk
Orders@xlibrispublishing.co.uk
305743

# CONTENTS

*Dedicated to Andrzej Kurpiel*

# WHITE SHEETS

An empty page, a vacant mind,
Ah! a feverish mind, if truth be
Told: nothing to tell, yet everything
To register deftly.

Deftly, yes, and simply, briefly,
To the point. If only I could gleam
Forth in my prime, yet here I am
Stuttering and fulminating at an
Empty page.

It refuses to be filled with words
Of worth, wise words, sober too.
Ye gods! why I must scribble here
This stormy night: a precise
Reflection of my soul this autumn
Night. And yet, I am addicted to
The task in hand, and to my
Daily dose of reading.

Like a boggy stream, I go on and
On: I cannot turn back. I bemoan
The loss of faculties which once
Gave me the edge. Staying yet
Again in psychiatric wards make
My writing so much less a thing
Of beauty, soft and sweet, such
As would make my Muse so proud.

I am deserted by my Muse, so
Much depressed deep down,
Counting days until my time
In Bedlam is done, and done
For good. Then I'll be resurrected
Once again, and my writing
Will show forth a newer Me.
Little consolation in my
Psychiatric lonesome grief,
maybe angels will bring relief.

The sheet in front of me
Remains pristine white,
Perhaps reflecting my inner
Self: do come, my Muse, and
Fill it up for me, this one and
Only time.

# BEDLAM

Wandering the corridors of Bedlam
Hearing shrill noises and screaming,
Some nasty business going-on, but
I'm not up to it to gauge the detail.
Too tired this day, so so tired, and
Worried and depressed. Away
From all I know and love, that
Grassy knoll where I engage with
Muses sweet: a mere memory now.
Staring, staring out the window
I see the world, a place cut-off this
Time, and of little consequence.
Confusion next my heart, and now
No appetite to engage the forces
That have brought me here. Oh!
That I may have the strength to
Face my fate this very hour,
Conquer demons deep within.
Give me happiness and freedom
So I can be renewed,
Incarcerated here no more. Take
These mental scars from off my
Brow, take these chains from off
My hands and let me sit on
Sunlit upper hilly fields and soak
The sun, and finally need this
Place no more. Farewell the
Freedoms guarded so, so
Jealously. I am disconsolate
This very hour, and wonder why
I'm here, destined to stalk the
Corridors alone.

# OLDER AGE

I'm older now, confused
At life's weird ways,
My memories are not
Precise, the way they
Used to be. My old
Acquaintances are
Dying one by one, a
Fate I hardly take
With ease. Yet I've
Got my gods and
Muse close by, to
Comfort me a moment
Still. In and out of
Psychiatric wards,
Composing still but
Not the way I'd like.
Existence so
Shambolic now, I
Live from day to day
And take it as it comes.
Autumn in my heart,
Winter in my soul.
For I would love to
Know all there is to know,
—But to what avail?
If only I could write a
Poem that would please
My Muse, a lasting poem,
Strong and true.
If only . . .

# MORNING

The soft September sunshine
Shining in my face, the crow
Is cawing in sheer delight at
Such an unexpected turn to
Autumn weather. Night-time
Empty street, deserted and
Forlorn, now a-buzz with
Rush-hour traffic in the
Blinding light. If we could
Have this sunshine inside
Our being all the time, Life
Would be so different.
Clear blue sky, happiness
Deep down inside: a
Momentary escape from
Deep depression in my soul.
When I have dealings with
My Muse, it's just like this
But now I am dejected for
She is far away. I cry out
*Come, sweet Muse!*
But to no avail. The sweet,
Clear morn' is left undone
For again I am alone. In her
Absence I shall soak the
Sunshine up, and drink the
Dew she left for me to make
Some *Poesy* divine. Not
Possible, of course, without
Her presence here and now:

A forlorn wish, as usual with
Me in my sunshine moods.

Morning, morning, happy in
The world: alas! for me, my
Muse I miss inspiring me to
Greater things with pen and
Paper this sober hour of
Morn'.

# HANGING-ON

Hanging-on by fingertips,
I'm in a low bipolar state,
Clinicians say I'm quite ok
Yet I know that's not my fate.
Others say I quite deluded,
While I know I'm not.
Truth is, I am hanging-on
By fingertips alone.
Hanging-on to sanity
Yet I am still quite sane,
The trouble is no one
Believes, what I am saying
To them. They, not me,
Have problems now, I'm
Quite happy in my way,
I'll always keep that
Happiness, no matter
What they say.

# BEDLAM'S LEGACY

How do you put on paper
The deepest feelings
Arising out of deep, deep
Depression? Folk, good
Folk, rarely understand
The situation fully.
The birds are chirping
Happily, the day is one of
Pure delight, yet deep
Within there's a feeling
Of dejection, an inner
pain, a selected grief
within my being. The
Very clouds weigh down,
to my inner core and
Deeper still, so I am
Numb. Bipolar is the
Name, they tell me,
Yet the sheep graze
Quietly, content.

Not me.

# THE CEMETERY

Grandma's grave, a solemn place
And time this sober hour,
Surrounded by the peace of Death,
Birds chirping on the yews, the
Inscriptions not wasting words,
The bare minimum.

We miss you dearly, *Babcia,* three
Years since that fateful day you
Left us. But you are not alone,
Especially this prudent day when
We are re-united at this pristine
Sacred space. A gentle breeze
Wafts freely in your space, and
We are full of memories.

Oh! *Babcia*, if we could but have
One hour together again, just one
Hour to share the joys of yesteryear.
But you are in a safer Place,
Rested after your lifetime's work:
What work, what pain . . .

A peaceful place, not lonesome
Now, trees swaying gently: the
Vibes, they give serene effects
As we tidy-up round about., and
Prepare to leave, in peace, our
Solemn duty done.

Birch trees shimmer their
Good-byes, swaying in sorrow,
Iridescent in their way, uniquely
Blending with our mood.

No great chestnuts here: just a
Few thin trees soaking-up the
Goodness of the lives lying
Underneath. Flowers and votive—
Lamps left safely in their place
We tread gently on this sacred
Ground, and weep good-bye.

I blow a kiss, gentle, soft and
Loving: just like you were:
Gentle, soft and ever loving.

# LOVING MYSELF

Loving here, loving there,
Loving everyone but myself,
I need to love myself much more,
And be more gentle with myself.
For I have so much love inside
It's spewing out like a tap left
Open wide, but being creative
Takes its toll. I drive myself too
Hard at times. It's time to
Re-assess, and take it easy
For the times I need that love
To pour it on my empty page.
For I have much to give, but
Sadly don't receive it in return.
Except when Muses come to me:
Then I feel the mutual loving time,
And the world seems fair . . .

# HOW TIMES CHANGE

All the times, the happy times, are gone
For I am older now and not so merry
As I used to be, much more introspective
Too, but happy in my writing and reading
Words, wise words, from Mahon and his
Kind. My Muse, sweet Muse, come now
To me and in my older age bear gifts of
Wise words in my soul, and I will gather
Roses smelling sweet for thee. Literary
Roses, by the woodbines: not only these,
But flowers of every kind, in return you
Will let me feel the Muse's scent wafting
Round about my pen, and I shall make a
Poem worthy of the Muses . . .

# FOR ANNE

Loving, kind and merciful:
That's the way you were
Until one fateful day
Death took you far from us.
My triplet sister dear, your
Ashes now lay softly in the
Irish soil, that consecrated
Ground I'd love to visit once
Again sometime. You and I
Had special bonds, not lost
And never will be lost through
The ravages of time. The
Lonely tree, bent with the wind,
Gives witness to the growth you
Gave to other folk: I will carry-on
That feat of high endurance.
There was an inner innocence
Deep, deep down inside your
Soul: I used to envy you and
That magnanimous spirit you
Espoused to one and all, to
Everyone round about.
Perhaps that's why you were
So popular. Individual blades
Of grass stand upright in the
Wind, a soft Atlantic wind, in
Witness to your upright spirit
And loving bravery in face of
Death itself, dear Anne.

# A LONE TREE

Brambles shaking wildly,
A lone bent tree bends
A fraction more, a very
Large bonsai, as it were.
Bruised and battered by
Atlantic storms, but
Hanging-on for life itself:
Gaunt, riven to the core.
If only it could tell of
Fiercer storms than now,
Yet stands witness to
Traditions eked into the
Very dust beneath. This
Irish soil so fertile,
Providing nutrients way
Down deep, they give
Nourishment galore to a
Tree so scrambled, in
This remote peninsula
So far from civilised ways.
Alone among the brambles
It steals the weather well.
I continue on my way,
Enhanced by my meditation
deep.

# A DEAR WISH

For I would fain pen a poem good,
And lasting down the good times
And the bad times: a poem worthy
Of the name, but oh! alas! 'tis
Something I can only wish for in my
Wilder self. Autumn's creeping on,
Stealthily and by degrees, I feel old
And tired, in need of sleep, instead I
Beaver on, in hope that one day I
Will pen something worthy of the
Muse.

Summer flowers display a
Worn look, the night-time's no
Longer blazing warm. The year,
Like me, is getting older, and
Showing signs of wear. But
Autumn has its charms, for
Sure, and the berries will
Shine forth against the leaden
Sky. Come then, I'll pen a poem
To match autumnal moods, and
Happy in my soul I'll be.

# NOSTALGIA

Nostalgia for the olden days,
When I was fit and young, and
Now I'm nursing in my mind
What might have been. My
Mind, so fragile, almost went
The way all roses go, but I
Was fortunate indeed, and now
I can recount the past without
any of the terror of recent years.
Seems the roses bloomed much
Sweeter then, but that's untrue,
Of course, just that my Golden
Age is drawing to a close these
Very days. I need the words to
Verify those moods: I have
Neither facts nor words, and
Yet nostalgia sticks like treacle
to my very core.

# DEW

Early September morn':
A heavy dew on everything,
The searing sun attacks the
Tree next-door, a luminous
Green turning to yellow fires
Off that lovely tree: I regard
It as my own. The rosebush
Soaked with beads of dew is
Pleasurable beyond words of
Mine this delightful early
Sunday hour alone, but not
Alone, for I commune with
Nature: we make a perfect
Match. The yellow roses do
Shine forth with mystic
Scent: my Muse is close at
Hand in my Garden of
Delights. Geraniums bring
Up the rear, small and
Wonderful to touch and get
The smell of leaves. That
Time of year again: conkers
Falling off the chestnut tree,
its signature *thud!* unmistakable.
Oh! September's dew, soaking
The world with its gentility . . .
The very stones are sodden in
Their isolation, sentry-like. And
I am happy, in my idiosyncratic
Way.

# HAPPY DAYS

Happy days and happy ways
Are few and far between

These ancient days of mine
As I grow older in my ways.

Arthritis gnaws its knobbly
way: rheumatism, too:

The poet is slowing-up
Imperceptibly.

Yet I am happy in my
Frame, deep in my soul.

The church spire sweats in
Early-morning mist as I

Meander with my stick: a
Slow walk round the block.

I have my books, my poems,
I have happy days.

# DEEP IN MY SOUL

Deep in my soul
There's a thirst

For beauty, for deeper
Thoughts than normally

I share, the pain is
sharp within my soul:

A Rembrandt darkness
Covers me about, though

Sun is shining on the
World, half-deservedly.

# SUDDEN DARKNESS

A mid-September evening,
And suddenly it's dark and
Dark within my being this
Hour. The birds have gone
To roost. Only the miniature
Millipedes are crawling
Underfoot, and they are few
Indeed.

Now a change of shift to
Lamplight reading, after tea.
No let-up on my reading: I
Have the patience of a
Beaver.

Long September night under
Lamp, come with my Muse
And let me have an hour of
Peace and double-concentration.

The cyclamen is perky, pink
And, modestly, shouting out
Its own unique delight at
Being alive . . .

# THE DAILY GRIND

Books piled up, papers
strewn about,
It's time to start another
day composing
Something grand and
fit for human
Consumption.

The urge is like the
migratory dance of the
wild geese as they
traverse continents in
total concentration.

But lo! It's not as easy
as all that, for too many
thoughts intrude. Which
is better: no thoughts
or too many?

The urge is primeval,
all-consuming to the
very core. The milkman
on his rounds, the
postman's running late,
I only wish that they had
time to study a poet's
fate . . .

# STAND AND STARE

Standing at my front gate:
Watching all the world at
My feet swiftly going
About the daily trek to the
Tube and the High Road.

Just like I used to do, but
Now retired I've more
Leisure to stand and stare.

Delightful September morn,
A searing early morning
Sun, gone the caustic wind
Of yesterday, the showers
Too.

Fag in mouth, stick in hand,
I am happy as I compose
Bits in my head for future
Times and future tomes.

# MY LEGACY

I want to leave a legacy
Of poetry sublime,
Sincere: it's all I have to
Give the world.
My poems, sincere and
Humble, are all I have
To give the world, for it
Is all I know. Oh! if only
I could pen a poem today
And leave the world a
Better place than when
My mother brought me
Here so many years ago.
Sometimes I cry with love
For a world destructed,
Sad: like I said before
I am merely sad, not mad.

# BEFORE CHRISTMAS

That time of year when the nights
Draw-in so suddenly, the long
Haul to Christmas without
Diversion: it's here.

We'll settle-in and stake our
Claim to long, dark nights
When all there is is plenty
In the dark: books to read,
Manuscripts to devour in a
Reading frenzy lasting all
Winter long.

Oh! the joys of winter
Nights! Come, come quick
And stay with me in my
Isolation, in this city
Bursting forth with folk
Mad rushing here and there.

Sitting by a blazing fire,
Snug all winter long,
I shall compose poems
Sweet: even a sad, sad song.

# INFERTILE GROUND

The roses bloom
Where noting else
Will grow, and how
They bloom!

Geraniums in their
Pots will soon
Migrate to my warm
Greenhouse for
The winter months.

In the midst of
Wintry desolation
I shall feed them
Well, stay company
With them through
The winter long.

The greenhouse
Bursting forth in
Spring, before that
Time of plenty
Growth I shall cosset
all my plants through
Snow and ice, and
Be happy in my time.

# BRIEF MEDITATIONS

Dodging between September
Showers I meditate about my
Fate in this fast-moving life
Of mine. I wander slowly,
Think aloud about Life's
Verities. For sure I'm
Slowing-up, but still there's
Much to give the future, sad
Sad though I feel while
Raindrops spatter me
Without apology or even
Due recognition.

# MY NEST

I've made my nest
Where I belong,
I love it, so I do. It's
The place I fly out
From every day,
Return to at night.
It's clean, spotless,
Full of strong twigs
And down. It's my
Little piece of the
World, I can call
My own. It's a
Prized possession
And the best bit
Is the library full
Of books of poems.
And the open
Fireplace, so warm
In Winter. For years
I wandered and
Visited the world and
Saw so many other
Nests of every kind,
Then one day I
Bought my very own.
I shall die here just
As I have lived here:
With pen in hand:
That, at least, is
My wish.

# STARING

Staring out the window
I see the rose-bed
Blooming, and meditate
Upon my simple, spartan
Room, a psychiatric room.
I'm far from home, lonely,
Incohate in my poetry
This time and hour, dour
In mood, hungry.
I am locked-in, diagnosed
Over and over. I rebel.
The rose below my window
Is my one symbol of love,
The roses never shone as
Beautiful as now, for me.
I'm ready to cry, but feel
it's unmanly. I rebel.
Geraniums galore,
Pristine in their innocence,
I love them all: if only those
In charge would let me
Fondle them and smell the
smell they give. I rebel.
Ye gods! that I may free
Myself and be among the
Birds chirping freely at
My window bare, dirty too.
My brain craves freedom.
Unresolved tensions in my
Brain, and sweat. I rebel.

# THE SONG OF THE WORLD

The song of the world
Is sad, though full of
Love, like the slow
Lapping of the waves,
Like a piece from Chopin.

The sad, sad song of the
World is deep in my soul
This early hour of day.

The song of the world is
Resonant all round, from
The busy pub to the
Spare silence of the owl.

The sad, sad song of the
World is vibrating all
Around, if we could but
Tune to its frequency.

This song is in my heart:
I want to spread it far and
Wide. I conclude that
Because it is full of love
The sad, sad song of the
World deserves to be
Described as HAPPY.

Happy is the song within
My soul, like the chirping
Of the birds, or the
Play-acting of the porpoises.

# CYCLAMEN

After a gentle sleep
A gentle poem lies
Within my breast.
The cyclamen: it
Cheers me up, so
Delicate and pink,
And perky, too.
Geraniums galore,
And roses smelling
Sweet. The cyclamen's
My favourite for its
Sheer gentleness.
Exquisitely so.
Perky, precious,
Pirouetting on my
Kitchen table as I
Write. Caressing the
Petals in my hand is
Pleasure indeed.

# COME NOW MY MUSE

Come now, my Muse,
And tell me what is
Wrong that you don't
Come to me of late. I
Need you to inspire
Me as I compose each
Day. But lately things
Have changed. I miss
You so. I need to
Climb the mountain one
More time, together,
Yet my arthritic leg
Forbids it. Let's play
In Happy Hunting
Grounds, the Fairies
Gathered round, and
Together we will
Make sweet music by
The woodbines in
That shady grove,
That grassy knoll
Near that waterfall,
By dimpled mushrooms.
Come *now* my Muse . . .

# THE JOURNEY

I am on an eternal journey,
Going, going, going without
Cease: when will I arrive?

I repeat bits of my journey
Inadvertently: it's time to
Reassess, and ask some
Hard questions.

I never asked to journey:
I was put on the train.
Later, much later,
I changed trains and am
Still travelling.

The journey is a mystery,
A wonder beyond my
Powers to describe.
Curiously, my fellow-
Passengers are equally

Abandoned to a fate
They cannot stop. We
Can and do find
Diversions on the way:
The journey is eternal.

Who's driving the train?
Who started the whole
Thing originally?
Why are there no
exceptions?
The journey is eternal.

The signal is always green,
We are committed.

# AM I A STRANGER?

Am I a stranger to myself?
Am I a stranger to my home
City? Intimacy, yet ignorance.
Familiarity, yet illiteracy. And
I try so hard to respond to
Everything new, but I am
Slowing-up. I am a
Stranger in my adopted
City, not only when abroad.
A stranger to myself, not
Only to those close to me.
In an attempt to familiarize
Myself with the detritus of
The past, I crumble the dust
of the old town In my hands.

But to no avail . . .

# MOANING

The moaning and the groaning
In my heart for love of yesterday,
And years gone by,
Is intensified these recent times
As I am getting somewhat older.
The love of my homeland
And of my adopted city is as intense
As ever, never to be lost.
But I am moaning in my heart,
Groaning for yesterday,
And summers years ago.
I see the beauty passing-by,
And know it won't be mine
For too long more.
I am moaning in my heart
For love of yesterday.

# FREEDOM

Sometimes in my heart I sing
The song of freedom.
Sometimes in my heart
The song of freedom dies.
I treasure my freedom
Where I live, and will take it
To the grave. The price we've
Paid for that precious freedom!
Sing the song of freedom:
Never let it die.
The wild geese are free to fly
Wherever nature urges them.
The shivering birches are free
And fascinate us with their
Shimmering foliage. I am free,
Within reason, to be me.

# BIRCHES

Since early childhood
I've loved the birch tree:
Then travelled through
Russia and became
Besotted by them.
Shimmering in their
Delicacy, the very
Scratched, torn bark
Speaks to the painter
And the poet.
They sing a music
Unique while they
Sparkle non-stop
For our pleasure.
They have the
Delicacy of a
Botticelli, not the
Darkness of a
Rembrandt. And
Yet they are patient,
Sturdy as nails,
Withstanding all
That nature can
Throw at them.
The peeling bark
Is shedding
Long-lost memories.
The birch tree is
My very own, in
All colours and
Seasons.

# ROAMING

There are times when I want
To go roaming in the hills
And valleys of yesteryear.
Now so much older, 'tis time
To stop for a rest, open my
Rucksack and enjoy my
Sandwiches. Time to bring-
Out my albums and peruse
My photos. Oh! that I could
Climb Ben Nevis one more
Time: alas, 'tis not to be . . .

# RETURNING TO IRELAND

Am I a tourist or an emigrant
Returning? I ask myself at the
Departure gate at Heathrow.
Nearly fifty years away, have I
Changed? I ask myself. Has
My homeland changed?
Sure I have, sure it has, I tell,
Reassure myself. The prodigal
Son has taken the bold step
That identifies him. I have
Relatives waiting, kisses,
Cuddles galore, and
A hundred thousand welcomes
At Shannon airport.
Happy in my heart, I bury
Doubts, insecurities as I
Answer the obvious questions:
*"And how are you?"*
*"Welcome home"*
Home? Home? I ask myself.
My home is over the hills and
Far away, but I know: once an
Irishman, always an Irishman,
And home is where the heart is.
Nostalgia takes over, and I want
To cry, my mouth is dry, I want a
Magners. And we head to the pub,
And that's what I get. There is love,
There is happiness, and I accept

I'm at home with loved ones.
Out of touch, I'm familiar with the
Poetry emanating from Ireland,
I'm in such mood I could recite
Chunks of it, but then my Muse
Is with me now and all is bright
deep within. Home? I'm an
Inveterate wanderer, and guess
I'll always have that in my genes.

But God! it's good to be home, I
Tell myself as we wander round
The nostalgic places of my
Childhood: as so often happens,
Little is said as I soak-in the
Warm memories of a happy
Childhood.

Yes, God! Good to be home!

# BLOWING IN THE WIND

The horse chestnut,
Shimmering and blowing
In the late September
Morning wind. And right
On cue, dropping its
Supply of conkers.
Enjoying the unexpected
Late Indian Summer, the
Flowers in my Garden of
Delight are putting on a
Late flourish. Caressing
The bark, it's as if I can
Hear the sap running
Through the miniature
Eco-system, for that is
What it is. Strong and
Durable, immovable, my
Heart is one with nature
This windy morn'. This
Tree will never die, it
Stands sentinel for
Generations.
Oh! Nature on my doorstep!

# THE WIND

The wind is tearing
Through the trees,
The trees sing
A specific sigh
Neither sad
Nor happy
And yet methinks
It's a song of praise:
A reminder of what
Goes on
Right before our eyes.
But we don't see or hear.
The wind on the face,
Blowing, a soft wind.
The trees delight the
Eye, but also the ears.
If only we could see,
And hear and smell.
The wind it swells
The ocean white, far,
Far from home upon
The land. The blades
Of grass bend in
Uniformity, before
The Westerly,
That all-consuming
Monitor of Nature.
The trees sing out
A rustling song, but
Who is listening?

The wind blows
Through the curtains
Of my mind: my mind
Is fresh and vigorous
And ready to write . . .

# NOSTALGIA

Nostalgia raises doubts
About the state
Of things: I cannot help
But think of yesteryear,
And all the good events,
Minus the pain and grief
When things went wrong.
I'm told nostalgia isn't
Good for soul or mind,
Yet I disagree and
Wallow in nostalgia quite
A lot. But within reason.
No rose-tinted glasses
Now, simply the wish
To re-live the Good Times
While my fading memory
Lasts.
Nostalgias' a gift from
The gods: no longer do
I have to live
On milk and honey alone . . .

# NATURE IN AUTUMN

Each blade of sweaty grass
Laden with dew,
Cold to the touch:
Am I all alone in noticing?

Each fallen leaf dancing
Down the street, rustling
In unison with its fellows,
Oh! the crunchy music
Made when I deliberately
Step on them,
It's autumn for sure
In London Town.

Each single flower
Packed tightly
In my greenhouse,
Each one
A miracle of creation.
There they will stay
Until the thaw of spring.

Each puff of wind
Tearing at the eaves
And in my
Idiosyncratic way
I love each movement
That same wind produces.

Each drop of gentle rain
Falls at a slow angle:
My plants will no more
Rot from excess of damp.

Each time I visit
My Garden of Delights
I marvel at what's
Before my eyes.

# THE STIGMA

The stigma of having
Mental health issues
Is painful beyond words.
Folk are suspicious,
Even aggressive, to
Those who otherwise
Are lovable. Having
Mental health issues
Myself, I am lovable.
Blow me a kiss,
Dear reader,
Treat me gently,
Open your mind
To the possibility
That every human is
Somebody's baby . . .

# A LONE POEM

I am a lone poem,
I will sit and wait
Oh! yes, sit and wait:
Wait, that is, until
You read me.

I shall survive,
Maybe even prosper,
If enough readers
Notice me.

So, dear reader,
Take me gently
Read me all over,
And see the Muse
In me.

I dread the bookshelf.
There I have to compete
With so many
Of my kind.

Please fondle me,
Take me to your heart,
And remember:
You may become
My very best friend . . .

# MINDFULNESS

It's the middle of the night,
Muses all around,
Spreading Mindfulness at
Me, and so I notice all in
Great detail. Relaxed, I
Put my pen to work, I
Read and read again
The favourites from my
Bookshelf. Retired, I can
Afford such luxury through
The night-time. How lucky
I am to have my Muse this
Special time. I notice
Detail I've missed before:
Mindfulness, relaxed
Completely in my literary
Task this happy hour.
Oh! that I could have this
Gift for e'er. Some wish.
Like a monk in the
Scriptorium I etch away
At the vellum: but caution
Warns: who am I to claim
Comparison with monkish
Genius?

# SUDDEN SHOWER

A sudden sharp, horrid shower
Disrupts my meditation in my
Garden, intimations of autumn
In the late September air. My
Plans are all disrupted now,
But *Hey!* the goodly times are
Deep within, for I've got books
Galore to inspire my eyes and
Soul. It's calm like a bowl of
Mercury today. Suddenly I
Notice, in the distance, a clear
Blue sky as if the shower lost
Interest and got bored, so now
Moved-on. There's a sheen on
Plants and droplets on the roses
White, yellow and pink. Noticing
The detail is joy indeed: the
Sudden sharp, horrid shower has
Done its job, and I am witness to
Its benefits.

# PAST TENSE

I must go to visit childhood sites
To keep the memory alive,
And greet the stones I trod on
In my youth: greet the fog that
Covered up my mind and vision
In those early days; greet the
Grasslands where we hunted
Foxes, renew the memories
I've stored these fifty years
Now gone. Where memory
Fails, nostalgia overtakes,
And I am so exited now at
The prospect before my eyes.
Distance dulls decidedly,
But Time unravels the cord
Of imprecision. Fifty years
Away from home, past tense
Indeed, and how I've changed,
These childhood sites have
Changed as well, no doubt.
But we'll get so familiar again
And I will feel complete inside.

# MIDNIGHT

Somehow in the
Midnight hour I
Contemplate
The best,

I host the Muse
And faeries when
All have gone to
Sleep.

There is a hidden
Poem waiting
to be born at the
Midnight hour.

The delivery is
Problematic
Sometimes, but
With my Muse
As midwife,

All is well.
Poet and poem
Are doing well.

# CONCRETE

Concrete underfoot,
Hard, unyielding,
Nothing like the
Gentle stuff on the
Many green roads
I traversed in my
Youth, or the
Mountain tracks
Of yesteryear.
But that is city life,
And as I get older
I find my arthritic
Feet are not up to
It. Gone are the
Days of yomping
Freely in the wild,
Watched by a
Golden eagle.
Farewell, farewell . . .

# IN TUNE WITH NATURE

When the sheep meander merrily
On open pastures, I have a joy that
Is unsurpassed.

Watching a goat chewing brambles:
Makes me so in tune with nature.

Noticing squirrels jump for sheer joy
Is beyond words.

Studying a ladybird on the hand
Brings inner peace.

Hearing the cuckoo makes me
Nostalgic.

Cuddling a labrador and seeing
Her response: total delight.

Scratching the cat's head and back
when she comes back for more
Gives me total serenity.

Concentrating on the millipedes,
The creepy-crawlies all over the
Flowers, keeps me young.

Seeing two cranes perform a
Courting ritual roots me to the spot.

Listening to the trees growing
Renews my faith in nature.

# LISTENING TO THE STONES

They are immovable,
The spaces between
Them fascinates me.
They have patiently
Absorbed so much
Of our history, yet
They remain silent.
Schist and mica
Quietly give way to
Nature's stronger
Forces, but in our
Blindness we
Cannot see. They
Change colour
During every shower.
Naked, they endure
Every extreme
Of climate. They
Graciously allow
Mosses and lichens
To hitch a ride
For eons. They
Have settled in such
Accidental patterns
Whereby the spaces
Are as interesting as
The stones themselves.
Lambs bleating nearby

Make the scene more
Idyllic.

I listen to these stones
With intensity: they are
More than a match for
Our times. The stones,
The stones, majestic in
Their structure and in
Their patience.
Silent, benign monsters.

Behold the silence
Of the stones.

# HOPE

Hope in a world racked by despair;
Hope in a world experiencing
Intense existential loneliness.

In spite of all the love;
In spite of all the fun;
In spite of all the hugs.

Incarcerated in the
Psychiatric Wing,
I am certain that hope
Is the best medicine
When all is hopeless
Round about.

Embalmed in my own
Personality, imprisoned
In my Unconscious,
The *Ego* and the *Id*
Fighting it out
Like two cats.

Hope is Faith: I believe
In my bowels that
Things will get better.

Hope is Faith and Love:
The love and respect of
Good and True friends
Who have stood
The test of time.

Hope in a psychiatric wing:
Too much to wish for
As I am assaulted by
A fellow-inmate.
Bruised, and in shock.
The head that once was
Caressed is now battered
In total despair.

And yet, and yet—
Hope there must be:
The alternative is
Too fearsome
To contemplate,

*Or so I think*
*In my deep, disconsolate despair*
*While I am locked away . . .*

# AUTUMN NIGHT

Dark, dark autumn night
Black as spades at five,
The clocks have just
Gone back one hour,
My summer's truly gone.

But we adjust, we will
Survive the shock.
Six months of darkness
In the offing. I love
The winter, for I read
Voraciously through the
Long, long nights.

Misty autumn nights
Serve us well, an aid
To meditative moods,
In romantic moonlight.
I notice berries, too,
As early fog evaporates.
Autumn draws me to the
Inner Man—a man
Refreshed by summer's
Glow.

Yet a man now growing old,
just like the year itself.
Mellowing. Mellowing
In silence, and reflection,
But not self-absorption.

The fallen leaves are
delightful, not a source
of pain; the leaves
not yet fallen,
Multi-faceted in their
Autumn grandeur,
Sing their song
Of dew-strewn innocence,
Offset the negativity
Of autumnal mists and
Darkness within the soul.

The autumn moon sheds
Light when all else fails
To brighten up my soul
This starry, stormy, silent
Autumnal night.

# ALL SOULS' DAY

All Souls' Day,
We visit *Babcia's* grave
And give her the respect
We give to all souls now
Resting the eternal rest.

Misty, moist, muggy
Clammy morning,
We are solemn but not
Morose, buying votive
Lamps and flowers.

She sacrificed her life
For us, now we
Sacrifice a day for her,
And gladly so.

Slowly, silently,
Soberly we move
This goodly day.

The trees stand silent
Sentinel as crowds pour
Past praying piously.
People on the move
*En masse,* in silent,
Solemn mood.

Meditating mutely,
Magic moments here
For me this holy hour
Of honour to the dead.

Pious people passing on
These rituals to younger
Folk, Heaven hears the
Heartfelt invocations, the
Mumbled murmurs,
Silent soliloquies stretching
All the way to
God's own Heart, this
Holy, heartfelt, honest hour
In Torun's teeming tide
Of goodly folk.


*Torun: a university city in northern Poland.*

# ANIA'S GIFT OF SOUL

A little bit of Soul is needed
To cope with Life's hard ways,
My soul is starved of emotion
And I am withering now, this
Very hour, alone, with
Writer's Block.

Texts from Ania cheer me up,
And she makes me born anew
For she's a dear, dear friend
To be counted among the few.

Oh! Ania, I do love you so,
The best friend I have got,
Soul you emanate in plenty
For Soul you have galore;
Pass it on, dear Ania,
Pass it on, for you are there
To give the world badly needed
Kindness, a lot of Soul . . .

# A NEWLY-BORN POEM

Like the bleating of a lamb
The new-born poem calls out
For the sustenance of added words
To enable it to grow and flourish.

Words it will get, but will they
Be enough? Will they guide
And nourish it through the
Difficulties of life in a hard
Commercial world?

I shall cuddle it, and
Nourish it, with good words,
Kind words, positive words,
The very milk of human
Kindness.

It will grow, and become a beacon
Of light to whomsoever . . .

# NOVEMBER

November: misty,
Mild and mystical,
Clammy, damp and
Full of fallen, famished
Leaves.

The trees are taut and
Naked now, standing
Silent sentinel, rooted
To the spot in frozen
Filigree, against the
Neon streetlights.

I trundle through the
Piled-up leaves,
Careful not to slip.

Bare and fully isolated
Now, stripped of summer's
Sumptuous growth, while
Then supporting summer's
Sprightly show,
The trees look gaunt,
Neglected, indicating
Truths about our sore
Predicament.

Time takes its toll,
And leaves aesthetic pain,
To view November views
Makes me think again
Before I rush to judge too
Soon.

Long days ago, the same
View was so different
And happy were those
Summ'ry days, now the
Mood has altered so,

Now drawn and bony,
Greedy for that summer's
Show, seasons make us
Change our view;

Stopping, staring silently:
The view just now is
Despondent, desolate and dour.

# NOSTALGIA

Nostalgic, I recall
The eagles's nest high above
The mundane needs of
Everyday: those were the days
When I would trek the wilderness
Without a thought for comfort or
Ability.

The blue, blue lake awash with
Furrowed skin, granite hills
Gaily garbed in gorse.

Now I'm in the wilderness again:
A wilderness deep inside my mind
—Inside my very soul.
The happy times of rambling
Now long gone, arthritis takes its toll.

Yet the memory of rambling times
Will cleanse my soul and bring a smile
To wizened face once more.

# FOR I AM NOW ALONE

For I am now alone,
Arthritis-bound, and
Recollecting days when
I would jump a fence
To reach another field.
Those days were days
Of vigour, strength and
Fulsome happiness,
Days of laughter, caring
Not for morrow's needs:
Living an eternal present
Without a need to think of
Future times, or care about
The past.

Full circle now I've come:
Chuckling I recall those
Carefree days. I am happy
In my memories, no doubt
Or negatives to blight
That happy state.

I gloried in the sunrise
As it tipped the mountain-top,
And bathed it in gold,
Then saw it dip again at night.

And now I am alone
But happy at the memories
So grand, my movements slow,
Deliberate and full of pain, but
Happy is the man who lived
The kind of Life I lived.
Happy man, indeed . . .

# CREATING

Creating poems is full
Of mystery, and when
The Muse comes by
The mystery is doubly so.

Because I cannot understand
Why one day I do write so well,
Yet other days the task is onerous
Indeed. The primeval urge to write,
To put on paper those immature
Ideas, notions, deepest thoughts:
This urge it is unbearable at times.

Creating is a fundamental joy,
Yet sometimes full of pain within.
I write at night when midnight
Strikes, and faeries come to play
With me in mystic glades where
Muses dwell. The early morning
Light is full of possibilities, look
And you will find me there waiting,
Watching, weaving words and words
Galore upon the empty page.

Deciphering the inner bits of wordy
Ways, the moon negotiating windy
Nights, I settle for a phrase that seems
To work, but ever wonder if a better
Poet might place another, better
Phrase instead, and say it all in
Finer style. Oh! mystic Muse, do
Come, inspire me now,
The moon is full
—and I create alone . . .

# THE EMPTY SHEET

*Facing the empty sheet makes me come out in a cold sweat, makes me*
*Wonder about the very vocation of the writer.*

The empty sheet it stares me back,
I am loath to mark it so, lest I spoil

A thing of beauty. Aesthetic
Happiness is mine when I see it in

Its nakedness, pristine white, and
Waiting to fulfill its destiny, nothing

Other than to be filled-up with words
Of wisdom for a generation still to
Come.

Where are the words?
Where is the distilled wisdom?

Not in my heart this ungodly hour, alas.
And yet there lurks a primeval urge to

Scrape the cave-wall with what we
Know: the mundane things impressed

On us from familiarity itself. The urge
To type a line, to tell a tale of everyday

Is all-consuming in my breast, devoid of
Artificial sentiment, instead some worthy

Words, worthy of the scribe's delight as
He scribbles in the margin just for fun.

And yet the vellum's not disgraced, yet
My wordy words pay deference to

Paltry efforts in the moonlight hour, while
Night-time foxes prowl outside, while cats

Do squat beneath the cars along the street,
Until the danger's passed.

The empty sheet is docile so, accepting
What is piled upon its virgin face, I kiss

The poem and send it on its way to weave
A thought or two to comfort readers still to come.

# CHRYSANTHEMUMS

Chrysanthemums
they blossom bright
in mid-November gloom:
sharp yellows, whites
show off the crystal vase
—they make a perfect match.

Symbols of nobility, bright
and cheerful they
maintain a happy watch in
moody times when all is
dark and dimness rules the
day.

And yet, they have an
underside in countries far
from here: representing
Death, and sorrow, too.

But I love the brightness
that they bring to gloomy
dismal, dreary days, petals
dropping off in silence as
I gaze in fascination,
every time.

# THE MIND

The mind, capricious ever,
resorts to stealth to make
another day worthwhile.
The world attends to what
it knows, the mind just
follows on, too naked and
too sensitive to bear the full
sunlight so early in the day.
Sunlight in my soul, methinks,
until I try to make a poem
there and then—and yet to
no avail. Too early in the day,
too late at night, and yet the
mind will force its way to tell
the page what pages need
to know. Pages, empty pages:
they cry out to have the mind
just have its way with them,
they are happy just to be
filled-up, be it churlish from
a churlish mind, or wisdom
rare, sublime. Even in the
midnight hour, the mind is
working still, in dreams: if
only we could master all the
mind's activities, and venture
forth with confidence to
measure minutes and the
passing hours, for all to see.
A broken mind is sad to see,
a tragedy should it be me

incarcerated here in Bedlam
one more time. The mentors
know the mind so well—and
yet they do not understand *my*
mind. And so I do resort to
stealth, just to survive another
hour, another day. I am locked
away, and will be for some time,
free no more to take a walk, to
roam the moonlit pathway for
fresh air. Moonlit moods, like
fog, assemble all around, but I
am happy, happiness doled out
frugally in these isolated parts. I
know my own capricious mind,
capricious is the mind in here that
strains to last, survive. Capricious
mind, that's me. Stealth: my newfound
wealth, in here in Bedlam sad.

# FOG

Four a.m. The fog envelops
All around outside, typical
November night.

My mind is clear inside:
Typical of me to be awake
This foggy time, all is
Silent round about, no
Cats, no foxes on the
Prowl.

Composing fiercely through
The misty haze: fascinating
Though, to watch the
blobs of mist descend and
Swirl round the street-lamp,
Silently descending,
Swirling round and round
At this unearthly hour.

Everything now's soaking
Wet, though not my soul
Or mind: for now my time
Has come to pen wise
Words, if come to that, with
Help from Muses fair, drawn
Gently from their lair in
grassy knolls in further
Fields where woodbine
grows.

Fairies, too, are near about
At this famished time. I am
A happy client of all the
Night-time sprites. Happy
Is the soul so full of
Origins in text that makes
It to the page this watery
time of night.

Oh! spirits of the night, do
Come and fill my mind
With textual delights and
I will see to it that we will
Make a Pact in secret ways
and thereby please my Muse,
And her craving for attention
Close to all her wishes dear.

# THROUGH THE NIGHT

I like being up
through night-time hours,
the solitude, the peace
engendered then
is something special
for a poet's craft.

The foxes scowling
round about, tail up,
the scribe who
scratches a paltry
life on parchment
which responds to
every scrape, so
gently placed, the
sound of nib on that
same parchment hard.
Scoring, scratching,
scraping vellum as the
monks used do in olden
times, but who will read
these midnight words,
these weasly, scanty,
stingy notes of mine?

The night-time dew
is falling imperceptibly,
the fog, the dreaded fog
encroaches nearer
still, and through the
night-time hours it does

its work, enveloping
each leaf with mastery.

This devious work adds
to the silence deep, and
in the early morning all
is soaked and sodden still.
And what a miracle of
nature to behold, before
the burning sun drains it
all away.

The feline world
is busy, too, as they pout
about, their concentration
a stark reminder to
distracted poets through
these night-time hours.
Soon the dawn will herald
yet another day, and I will
take to bed to rest a
febrile mind and soul.

Give me night-time hours
galore: that is who I am.

# INCARCERATION

My brain incarcerated
still, my brain a prisoner
of habits nasty, bad.
I want the freedom of
the Good, and yet
depression lurks about,
too near for comfort
now, as I ponder my
predicament prior to
entering the psychiatric
ward again.

Oh the pain, the pain,
the disappointment
too, just when I thought
all was well, and happy
times were bound to
come to furnish me with
happy hours: all to no
avail.

I face the prospect now
of weeks away from all
familiar things, Bedlam's
standards now will be the
norm for days and weeks
ahead, as far as one can
bear that prospect grim.
Days of regimented drill,
stipulation quoting rules
and regulations stark.

Screaming violence, to
boot, and no escape
—not even walks in open
air, the very windows
locked, in case I jump.
Caustic looks, and
nothing said: all I can do
is bear it grimly, and be
as obstinate as they.

My brain indeed
incarcerated
to the point of stillness.
I adopt a Zen-like
compliance, in order to
survive: to survive is all
I'll do these next few
days and weeks.
Dear reader, think of me
in my incarceration,
full of drugs and psychiatric
verbiage. For I am deep
depressed and think of
better ways to treat
my sore condition now.
Those better ways they
won't adopt, even
though it's best for me.

Survival: how can I survive
or even prosper when
there's no more time to still
compose my poems, but
time I'll find, and I'll
compose ferociously in
my Zen-like trance, alone.

Ye gods, that I may know
the strength that
incarceration brings if I use
it craftily and wisely, too.

I am truly now alone, listening
to the chorus that the
screaming and the fighting
brings to famished ears: oh!
to hear the choral symphonies
and Chopin, but no, alas, alas.

And as the savvy spider
weaves a web outside, with
patience still, and then
withdraws to wait, I am
inspired indeed in my lone
room, glad to follow
nature, while all the while
rejecting all the nurture
proffered me, for I know
I'm sane, simply now
depressed somewhat.

Why did I say the things
I said that led me to
this place, this time?
Ne'er again, I promise,
just let me now survive
alone, sparse room
and all that. For sure I
will survive this Bedlam
place, and prosper—in my time.

# DIGGING, *Heaney-Style*

The poet digs deep
decidedly—deep
to the unconscious
mind, if need be now.

Maybe pearls way
down deep: pearls
of reality that escape
the daily din; dour
distractions that
prevent us being
alive to all the vibes
that make us whole.

A gem of wisdom
rare, perhaps. to
comfort 'midst Life's
brutal cares: pain
within the body deep,
and deep within the
brain.

Insights pertinent and
sharp, fill the poet's
life, perhaps, this very
hour. I see the inner
workings of the soul,
perhaps a sense of
Godness, too. The
bell it tolls a call to
morning prayer in

foggy distance way
beyond. Arthritic legs
don't walk that far, yet
in my soul I pray.

I am betrayed by
monkish traits as dawn
delivers daily dew, to be
seen and studied by the
few. The poet's sense of
light Divine is yet another
gem quite rare.

I dig the page like Heaney
did—and find a gem at last,
deep, deep down beneath
the ground.

# UNFINISHED BUSINESS

The poet's work
is never done.
Happy is the man
who knows the work
of ancients gone,
who delves into the
inner ways and
workings of what it
is to see, and know,
and love.

Though the work is
sometimes grim, and
people tell you
*Get some sleep!*
the end result is worth
it all: perceptions
rare and goodly,
crowd around the
mind with mindfulness.

On dull December days
the fog is lifted when I
start to use my quill
and beaver-on,
merciless, and surly,
sour, sometimes.
That determined mood
is so important now,
the discipline of

early-morning scribbling
on the margins of my mind.

It gets me in the mood to
register the workings of a
life undone.
And when it's done
—it's never done entirely.

# SILENCE

In these testy times
the world's in
a frenzy,
—deep inside
my mind
is space for
total silence
in the early
morning hour.

I study cobwebs
close at hand,
clammy,
quivering.
The morning
dew is
everywhere,
the cockerel
wide awake,
heralding
another day.

Like a Trappist
monk I read
my script, and
search for
just one word
to make it
all complete.

The little
birds are
chirping mad,
and glad to
be alive. As
they search for
nourishment,
I continue
still the search
for perfect
words.

Dreary, dull
December days:
but like the
birds my heart
is full of joy
at being awake
this early hour.

# SILENCE, 5a.m.

Early morning
meditative mood,
Spatterings of
rain upon the
window-sill,
the postman's
on his way to
work, and the
world is snoring
still.

Rivulets of rain
run down the
window-pane,
secretly, silently,
racing each other
fast. I can hear
the wind on the
eaves, howling,
howling, growling
too.

And suddenly it
stops, total
silence, broken
by the distant whine
of jumbos heading
hurriedly for
Heathrow, from
the Far East.

And I am
beavering away,
creating absolute
stillness in my
early exercise
this quiet,
happy hour.

# MORNING THOUGHTS

The soothing sense
of silence, still, in the
springtime morning sun.

Monks meditate
mindfully
while the world gets
ready for another day,
to survive—or even
prosper.

And I am working on
another poem this
early hour, while
folk around are fast
asleep.

Morning thoughts
are mainly in a
meditative mood.
I'm groggy from a
deep, deep sleep,
but thrilled to be
awake this hour,

glad to welcome
endless possibilities.
The day is mine to
give, and to receive
gratefully, for to give
is to get.

The day ahead is
mine to keep, all
for myself, up to
me to make of it
what I will.

From the brink
of suicide, in a
psychiatric ward,
it *will*
be good and
positive, full of
possibilities
for good and
goodness, and
goodly deeds.

*This is my post-suicidal legacy . . .*

# WORDS

So many words,
so few ideas,
so few words
to fit the many ideas.

Ideas thrown about
as the moon is
crystal clear at
ten to two, the
pain inside the brain
at lack of comprehension.

Disorganised and fidjety
I play with words
to no avail, I drill
inside the mind
for better words
fit to grace the page
this demon-hour
of night.

The foggy dew
this winter night
becalms a fretful world,
becalms a consternated
mind: alarm and
panic rule the soul
as I search for words
to fit the notions
in my mind, but
to no avail

this fretful winter's
night, alone.

Words keep coming
to my mind, but not
the words I seek
to fit the purpose
of my wordy plan.

The gods torment me
at this lonely time. The fear
of failure looms so large,
and yet I know the poem,
new-born now, will
emerge full-blown to
greet another day,
some hours hence.

Words: patience.

# BIRTH OF A POEM

Crystal clarity supreme:
surpassing previous
doubts, for now my mind
is full of certainty.
In Bedlam's bleak
backwaters, screaming
down the corridor
—I know that I will
gain my mind again,
certain that the world
will be what it once was.

But not just yet, for
much work needs be done,
to survive such hellish
nights while others
sleep the sleep of angels
sweet.

A punch-up down the
corridor before the
midday lunch distracts me
from my concentrated
mind upon a new-found
poem from deep within
my breast.

Drugged full of strange
psychotic cocktails, I
barely manage to recall
the task at hand.

Safety rests in being alone
within my bedroom walls,
entry none, exit none, and
staff keep banging but
there's no response from me,
pleas unheard, for my
poem is being born this
very hour.

Antisocial now, perhaps,
and yet my soul is full
of peace, for I am safe from
lounging louts who loiter
round about and want a fag
from drugged-up souls
like me.

My Muse and I have
deep affairs, and I know
deep down within that I am
on the mend provided I can
keep my dignity alone.

As psychiatric units go,
this isn't too, too bad,
the screaming and the
shouting do disturb my
very soul, and make me
shake with fear, sometimes.

My suicidal stance is o'er,
for now, an all-pervasive
existential loneliness as I
try to comprehend what's
going-on within the
mechanisms of my mind.

Existential angst is
all-pervasive now, as

another scream refrains
from near at hand.
My Muse has left
quite suddenly
as I negotiate my way
to lunch. Gastronomy
is not my wish this
paltry time, I want to walk
around the grounds, but
that is simply not allowed.

The lunch is wholesome,
nothing grand, and
straightaway I close my
door and, pen in hand,
I opine at length upon
my sentence long,
never-ending here.
Ye gods! give me
the strength to bear this
time from home, for
I miss my books
home-comforts and
the rest.

Those who think I can
be cured within Bedlam's
walls today, are misguided
folk, and I shall make a run
for it if kept like this: my soul
is chained. The chirping bird
outside is free to tell the world
its tale of joy, but here I am
incarcerated and unfree
to be myself. Three weeks
to go before I roam my
local streets, treated with
full dignity, seen as normal,
just as it really is.

Philosophies of life mean
nothing here, mere
survival is the rule, yet
I can't survive this mad
regime much longer now
in my present state.

Dear reader, take me
in your arms and assure
me all is well, or will be so,
soon, so soon.

The contradiction's there
for all to see: the so-called
madness in the brain and
originality within the breast.
*Jesus Christ* help me to
bear this crucifixion time,
my poem is born 'midst
gruesome pain, yet
when I read it, fully-fledged,
my happiness is all complete,
ignoring further screams nearby.

# SOLITUDE

Solitude and silence:
the wise man pondered both
and sourced his wisdom from
these wells of limpid,
splashing water in the
early hours each day.

Active, both: no mere absence
of the noisy, bawling crowd.
Solitude and silence:
Active agents, both.
Signposts on the rocky road to
wisdom pure.

Misty morning meditation
—perhaps a poem
might emerge full of purity of
purpose, that will bring delight
to souls far away from here.

Perhaps . . .

# WINDY DAY

A lone bird
riding high the wind
on a blustery
December day.

A lone soul
riding high
the dark night
of the soul.

Pity me as I
try to make
some sense of
this in the dark.

All is becalmed
within my being,
dry within
my soul.

I search for
satisfaction
to no avail, this
foul December day.

I cannot fly.

I cannot fly, alas.

# STORMY NIGHT

I wake-up suddenly,
and notice droplets
on the windowpane.
A gale outside: deep
deep peace within,
at ten to five.

The drops cemented
to the pane reflect
the stars above
as the moon emerges
from a massive cloud,
to shine upon
humanity asleep.

I see it clear, before
it's lost again. This
stormy night
unsettles naked trees:
I hear the rattling of
the wind upon the
eaves.

Inside, and cozy,
snug, I ponder many
things, reflect upon
life's windy ways,
way deep within the
soul.

One hour later, I
emerge unscathed
from my musings
deep: keen to face
another stormy day
this mid-December
time. Dark and
gloomy it may be,
yet my soul is
fervent, wide awake
to face another
storm again.

This is my strength,
my optimistic mood
this windy hour.

Wild and windy
weather, but not
inside my soul.

# SILENCE

A grey, dull dry December day,
The violent windy weather has
Left us all becalmed. Utter
Silence pervades the house,
Like the aftermath of Hiroshima.

Silence is all, my closest
Friend. It is full of
Possibilities. It is active, full of
Life, of potential wisdom, if the
Climate be right at the appointed
Day and hour.

Ah! the grey, dull dry December
Day, the kind of day when all I
Want to do is write, and feel the
Weight of every word, with
Pleasure and with inner strength.
I hold the every word up for
Inspection. The reader is my judge,
My silence is complete, this
grey, dull, dry December day.

# STAMINA

My strength is gone
from writing long into
the night, but not so
gone that I must leave
it now. I'll leave the
book when it is done,
in silence and in
solitude—until then
I'll work ferociously,
and happy, too, for
way inside is pleasure
deep: the source of all
delight.

I plough my lonely
furrow in the dark, lit
by the moon, the
sparkling stars guiding
me along. A moonlit
night is perfect for
a solitary walk, a
ramble in the dark,
guided by the need for
nourishment
within the mind:
reflections deep on
life itself, its inner
meanings for the here
and now.

Energy renewed,
fresh air in my lungs,
I come relaxed to my
long task, and soon
the dawn will greet
my work, and pay
deference to my
stamina.

# DETERMINED MOOD

Determined
In the early morning
Hour to hone a poem
To please the Muse;

Feisty 'midst the
Shimmering
Cobwebs, sticky,
Enveloped in
Beads of dew,
I wander slowly
With my stick,
Prodding the
Damp pathway in
Determined
Strike after strike.

In doing so, I
Stake my claim to
Solitude and silence
Deep; determined
To find solace on a
Clammy wintry
Morning, like the
Monks of old who
Wandered off,
Itinerants to the end.

Determined now to
Make this day my own,
Determined still to

Praise the gods and
Watch the Faeries
Go to sleep, fresh
From cavorting in the
Glades where Faeries
Play.

Far from being alone,
I share the company
Of Muses smelling
Sweet, the scent is
All-encompassing
And I am happy in
The damp, determined
To find solace in my
Idiosyncratic way.

Lately moved from
Psychiatric wards, the
Freedom is intense
As I sniff the wintry
Air alone. I am
Determined now:
Never was like this
Before. I dreamt of
This, the freedom
To be *Me*, when I was
Locked-up way inside
An Institution glum.

*Ye gods!* that I may
Stay this way.
I whisper to myself
The mantras as of old,
The cat is scurrying
Under a car—it, too,
In total silence, now
You see it, now you
Don't.

When incarcerated, I
Did pray for just one
Hour of freedom just
Like this, and now I
Am at peace,
Determined to enjoy
Such times as this.

Determination has
Paid-off.
Determination to
Succeed when all
The doctors kept
Saying *No!*
They refused me
One small walk,
Was I such a
Criminal?
They know not
What they do, in truth.

And now? I'm master
Of my life, and I,
Determined to the last,
Will use each day to
Foster goodly habits
To keep my mind
Quite sane.